Contents

Some words are shown in bold, **like this**. You can find them in the picture glossary on page 23.

Which animals have fur?

Mammals have hair or fur.

Mammals are animals that give birth to live young. Mammal mothers make milk to feed their babies.

Different mammals have different types of fur.

Monkeys are mammals. They have fur over almost all of their bodies.

What is fur?

Fur is a thick coat of hair that grows over the body.

It is made from the same **material** as your skin and fingernails.

Fur can be long or short.

It can look patterned or plain.

It can feel soft and fluffy or coarse and wiry.

What is fur for?

Fur is like a coat or a woolly jumper. It helps to keep mammals warm.

Fur traps air next to the animal's skin. This air warms up and keeps the animal warm.

These Japanese macaques live where it is very cold and snowy.

They have long, very thick fur. They can fluff up their fur to trap more air.

Does fur keep mammals safe?

For animals that live outside all day, fur protects their skin from sunburn.

Fur also protects animals from bites, bumps and scrapes.

This woolly monkey lives high up in the trees.

Its thick, soft fur protects it from scratches and insect stings.

Does fur help mammals hide?

Most animals have fur coats that help them blend in with their surroundings.

This tiger's stripy fur helps it hide in long grass. It can creep up on **prey** without being seen.

This monkey has grey and brown fur.

This helps it to hide in the trees from **predators**.

How else can fur help mammals?

Some mammals use their fur to send a message.

When this deer is scared, it flicks its white tail. Other deer see the flash of white and know there's danger.

When this monkey is in danger, its long hair stands on end.

This makes it look bigger and helps scare away an attacker.

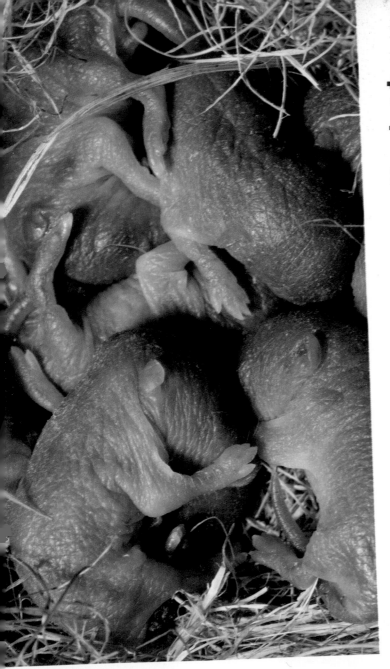

Are mammals born with fur?

Some mammals, including monkeys, are born with thick fur.

Other mammals, like these mice, are born with no fur. Their hair starts to grow when they are a few days old.

Some mammals have only thin fur when they are born.

A mother rabbit pulls fur from her own tummy. She puts this in the nest to help keep her babies warm.

Why does some fur change colour?

This baby deer has a spotty coat that helps it stay hidden in long grasses.

As it gets older, it will lose its spots and grow a thick new coat for winter.

Leaf monkeys are born with bright orange fur.

This makes it easy for their parents to keep an eye on them.

How do mammals take care of their fur?

It's important for mammals to keep fur free from pests, such as fleas.

Fleas are tiny biting bugs. They live and feed on the blood of larger animals, making them weak or sick.

flea

Monkeys check each other's fur for pests. They comb the fur with their fingers.

Monkeys can find it very relaxing!

Fur quiz

Which of these images shows monkey fur?

A

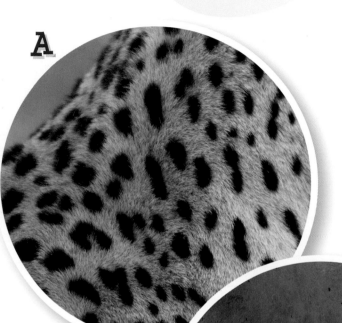

B

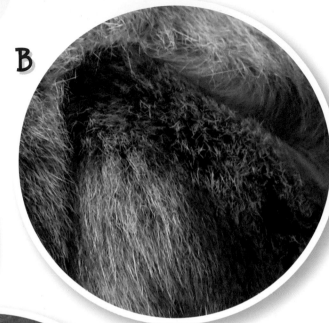

C

Answer: B

Picture glossary

 **material**   substance from which something is made

 **predator**   animal that hunts and eats other animals

 **prey**   animal that is hunted and eaten by predators

Find out more

Websites

www.bbc.co.uk/education/clips/zgwkjxs
Discover different types of monkeys.

www.bbc.co.uk/nature/life/Mammal
Meet the mammals and find out why they are
so successful.

Books

Marvellous Mammals, Isabel Thomas (Raintree, 2013)

Monkeys (Living in the Wild: Primates) Claire Throp (Raintree, 2012)

Why Do Mammals Have Fur? (Wildlife Wonders), Pat Jacobs
(Franklin Watts, 2014)

Index